T0209942

A Memoir of a Somebody

Mary Hart

WestBow Press books may be ordered through booksellers or by contacting:

WestBow Press
A Division of Thomas Nelson & Zondervan
1663 Liberty Drive
Bloomington, IN 47403
www.westbowpress.com
844-714-3454

Scripture taken from the King James Version of the Bible.

ISBN: 979-8-3850-1010-3 (sc)
ISBN: 979-8-3850-1009-7 (e)

Library of Congress Control Number: 2023919424

Print information available on the last page.

WestBow Press rev. date: 10/11/2023

Dedicated to innocence lost.

Introduction

A few years ago, I stood up in front of my Christian congregation and gave my testimony. I am naturally an introverted person so I find public speaking especially difficult. However, I imagine it would be difficult for anyone to open the closet and show the skeletons stored inside.

After I finished speaking, the pastor's wife talked with me in private and explained how I needed to put my testimony in writing and share it so other people could read it. She explained that it could possibly save someone from a life of darkness and chaos.

Ever since then, I have written my testimony several times, only to wad it up and throw it away. (Yes, the first several drafts were handwritten.) I then bought a laptop only to write it a few more times. It is difficult for me to show what I feel is my vulnerability. In my mind, if I do show my weaknesses to the public, I may be gossiped about, ridiculed, or even sneered at. Another reason is I do not feel I am a good writer, so who would publish my words? But here I am.

One day as I was going back and forth on writing this book, I came across a Christian motivational speaker on the television. As I listened to this person (I can't recall who he was), the words he was saying began speaking to me. Among the subjects he was teaching the audience, one gave me a bit of hope or maybe a bit of optimism, if you will. It was that you never know until you try. And the other was the first time the speaker wrote a book, the publisher sent it back and said to rewrite it. The speaker could have thought, *I am not a good author, and no one is ever going to publish anything I write let alone read any of my books.* Instead, he said, "Okay, where do I need to make changes?" And he rewrote his first book. He listened to the instruction. Now he says he has several books, some of which have been on the bestseller list.

I still have reservations about my ability to convey my thoughts on paper. My optimism comes and goes. When I start second-guessing, I ponder on what the speaker said, and it gives me the courage proceed. I am rewriting my testimony and pray it helps someone to come out of the darkness.

As I said earlier, it is not easy for me to talk about me, especially when it comes to the time I became broken. It is rather frightening for me to tell about some of my travels through life when I have made many mistakes. While I have many good decisions, it was not without falling flat on my face and listening to the derogatory remarks from people who want to gossip. It takes much effort at times to get back up and try again.

This book focuses on a specific part of my life, the time my spirit was broken and how my life spiraled out of control. I want the reader to understand how dark my life became, the depression it caused, and the many mistakes I made. I also want to show the triumph and forgiveness not only of myself but also of the person who caused the trauma. I am winning against the darkness; the fog has lifted. I hope I can show how God helped me to heal me.

My path has not always been easy, and I am sure there were many ways, possibly easier ways, to get to where I am, but this was the way my path went. The first thing to realize is I had problems. I was making bad decisions due to these problems. I also saw I was not taking responsibility for these bad decisions. I had to start being responsible for all my actions, the good and the bad. It was imperative I start seeing my life filled with blessings. This was when I started changing my attitude toward my life. I said all that just to say when I changed my attitude, it helped me to be grateful for all I have.

Once I was able to recognize my issues and began taking responsibility, my attitude and gratitude toward things gave me the tools I needed to conquer my bigger issues and my bigger fears. It is said, "A journey of a thousand miles begins with just one step." Some of those steps were not easy, but I had to make them to heal and have a better life.

I could not have made the first step of this journey without first listening to God and asking for His help.

Remember you are a somebody, you matter, and you can heal.

Thank you.

Mary Hart

Chapter One

In order to truly know where someone is going in life, one must first understand where that someone came from. Go back to the source of the hurt, of the pain, and of the trauma. The beginning where the person's life changed, where their world came crashing and turned upside down. We need to see where the source of the destructive behavior spawned. Then and only then can we understand why a person is where he or she is. Then and only then can we begin to offer hope to this person to understand where their issues came from and possibly show them the path to healing. If we can find the point in time of brokenness, then we can spark understanding for why a person is the way he or she is.

Instead of standing in condemnation of a person out of control, we should strive to understand the following:

- Why does one become an alcoholic?
- Why does one become a drug addict?
- Why does one have an attachment disorder?
- Why does one self-loathe?
- Why does one self-mutilate?
- Why is a person mad at God?
- Why does one decide to become an atheist?
- Why does one become an abuser?
- Why does someone become homeless?
- Why does one become an abuser or become the victim of abuse?

The list goes on and on.

Let us be clear. We as a society need to understand there are four psychological facts that God has instilled in us all, and they are the following:

- We like to be liked.
- We love to be loved.

- We want to be wanted.
- We need to be needed.

We were created to be interdependent beings. God made us that way. He also wants to be accountable to one another as well as to protect and care for our children. So when one of the above free-flowing energies becomes clogged with trauma, we become out of balance and thus become spiritually damaged or broken. And this often causes depression and can thrust us into a thick fog of chaos.

We need to love one another, care for one another, protect one another, and be accountable to one another. We need one another.

When we become out of balance and fall into a sea of darkness, we will seek to be liked, to be loved, to be wanted, and to be loved in any way we can, even if it means finding it in the most negative or unhealthy ways.

Many people are so far removed from God and the balance He has created in us. Most times, these people do not even know what they are doing is wrong or unhealthy. They do not know why they are the way they are, nor do they know why they are doing the things they do.

We also need to realize the brokenness, or the trauma may have happened when a child was so young that they cannot consciously remember it. It will remain in the subconscious or the psyche and cause many issues.

Satan loves imbalance, he loves chaos, and he loves sin. All of this keeps us separate from our Creator. If Satan can keep us from being born, that is all the better cause he has succeeded in killing the future children of God. But if he cannot do that, he works hard to damage the children, and the younger he can get to them, the easier it is for him to keep us away from God's loving arms—and the stronger of a hold Satan has on our lives.

You must realize Satan cannot know what is in the mind of God. It is when the Word is spoken that the devil goes into action. It was not until the Magi visited King Herod did the plan go into play to kill the male children in Bethlehem. Since King Herod did not know when the Messiah was born, he ordered his soldiers to kill all male children two years old and younger.

In the above instance, the "devil" came in the form of a king seeking to devour. The devil or Satan can *and* will come to you in many disguises. Instead of unseen forces as we see in a horror movie, he often uses people to do his work of destroying God's children.

Condemnation, however, should *never* enter our hearts, minds, or spirits when we see someone spiraling out of control. Instead, we should show compassion, mercy, and love. If we do not have the tools to help a person understand and to help them heal, we need to either find or pray someone can come into their lives to help with the acknowledgment of their chaos and to show the path to healing.

Yes, prevention is the best medicine, and if we lived in a society where we were balanced and where we could protect one another, that would be awesome. But oftentimes it is too late and we must pick up the pieces of trauma whatever they may be. Of course, if the person can get help soon after a trauma, the better it is for them to heal, thus leading to somewhat a normal life. Think of when someone breaks a bone or has an accident and gets a deep laceration on their body. The quicker they go to a doctor, the easier it will be to heal. A scar will be there, but the trauma will be minimized. The longer we wait, the more costly and the harder it will be for us to get better. The scars will be broader, and the pain from a re-broken bone is often way more painful than the original break. Not to mention if the person must spend time in therapy.

I know some people believe I am comparing apples to oranges with the above example, but hopefully you get the picture.

I would like to tell you a story. This is a true story of a little girl who had all the love and security in the world. Then that world came crashing down when she was raped at seven years old. This is a story of what she went through, the ups, the downs, the tears, the laughter, and how she went from rock bottom, depressed, and self-loathing to finding the light of forgiveness. This could be your mother, daughter, sister, granddaughter, niece, or even your grandmother. It could even be you.

This little girl is me, and even though I did not realize it until years later, God was with me the whole time, just waiting. I even asked where He was many times but was too caught in the fog of chaos to hear Him. I did not know how to listen. From my birth until now, God has seen me in my life's trials and tribulations and, yes, even the trauma of rape.

Nobody understands the pain, depression, the outbursts, or the acting out *except* those who have experienced similar traumas.

We are not nobodies! We are each a somebody, and together, we can heal!

Chapter Two

Coming into this world was not easy. I am my mother's first child. And she had a hard time when it was time for me to be born. She lay in labor for three days before another doctor examined her and prepped her for an emergency cesarean. Mother and I stayed in the hospital for a week after I was born. I weighed over nine pounds.

When Dad married Mom, he moved her to west Tennessee, to the Mississippi River bottoms to farm. Mom was from the hills of middle Tennessee, and she hated living in the flatlands. So when I was born, we moved back to middle Tennessee, close to Mama's parents. I am the oldest grandchild on my mother's side of the family, and I spent quite a bit of time with my maternal grandparents. They were simple people, they made use of their four-acre farm. They gardened and had chickens, goats, pigs, all to put away for food. I loved going to their house as a child. Granddaddy had a work mule named Jack Rabbit who was so gentle, I could ride him.

My grandparents were also God-fearing people and went to church every Sunday, studied their Bible daily, and prayed when they rose in the morning, when they went to bed at night, and at every meal. They would talk with me and as an inquisitive child, I would ask many questions. When I was about four years old, my granddaddy told me I was a special child of God and that our heavenly Father had a special job on this earth for me to do. He told me to always pray and believe God. I believed my granddaddy. He was one of the smartest men in my world.

Remember that when we speak prophesy over someone, we need to be careful. It did not matter how godly my grandparents were, the devil heard what was said, and a few years later, he came to destroy me.

When I was at the tender age of seven, the devil came to visit me for the first time. I was molested, or rather raped, by a much older man. He was a man who was trusted by my family. This man violated me several times between the ages of seven and nine years old. The devil uses many disguises to come as an angel of light to destroy. He came to me in the disguise of a fifty-something-year-old man. The devil knew the earlier he could break me, the more apt I would be to do his work instead the work of God.

He came to me quietly so no one would hear. He brought chaos to my peace; he made me fearful of my own shadow. He told me what we had was special and if I told my parents, I would be blamed and would be in trouble. He even visited me in my dreams and when he did, they were turned into nightmares. This was a horrific chaos I would not know how to fix for many years. I even started wetting the bed.

I was a shy child, unassuming with big brown eyes and short dark hair, who loved to read and loved nature. I would often take walks in the forest around my childhood home. I would sit quietly for hours and marvel at the animals and everything else in nature. I found out later that my shyness made me an easy target for this abuse. I was scared. I also did not have words at the time of the abuse to explain what was going on.

Statistically, one in three prepubescent girls are sexually molested (raped), and at seven years old, I became part of that statistic. I even remember what I was wearing: a little blue-and-yellow plaid dress with a white collar. I did not understand what was going on. It first started with him wanting me to sit on his lap, then he wanted me to kiss him. I kissed him on the cheek, but that is not what he wanted. This is how it started with me. I started out smiling, and I ended weeping. He told me not to cry, that this was a special secret that he and I shared and gave me some candy. He said that no one would understand and to keep it all between us. The physical pain I endured those few years paled in comparison to the spiritual, emotional, and psychological pain that would cling to my soul for years to come.

Most abusers are not strangers; they are someone known and trusted by the family, often a family member.

If being raped between the ages of seven and nine was not enough, a week before my ninth birthday, a female relative, my aunt, was murdered. The year was 1973. The murderer's intent was to first rape her, then kill her. Long story short, they fought, and she was shot by her own gun while her two-year-old and three-year-old sons watched. But she was not raped.

This was devastating to our family. I was already a quiet child who was being raped by an old man, then this happens. I became more frightened. I kept wetting the bed and did so till I was about twelve, and my fear and nightmares became worse. I would cry for no apparent reason. My family surmised it was all because of my aunt, but that was only part of the reason.

The *only* positive that came out of her death was that my rapist stopped abusing me. The damage, however, had already been done.

It seemed the devil was working overtime to destroy my family, not just me.

This was when I remember depression's roots had started sinking deeper into my soul. This was also when I first heard the devil's words speak to my spirit.

"You let that man touch you, but your family member would rather die."

"How can God love you now?"

"Your granddaddy lied; you are not special."

"You are a bad girl."

"You have never been good."

The little demons of depression, low self-esteem, and self-loathing began to grow in my young mind like kudzu grows and chokes out trees. They stayed for many years. As those roots grew, so did my chaos. A fog started to form, and it got thicker until I began to lose my way. These demons continued whispering until I let them take my hand and guide my steps.

Not only did this rape ricochet my life in a different direction but it also distorted or perverted my view of relationships, both friendships and intimate encounters, and really messed up what love and sex were supposed to be like for me. What I thought of family was extremely messed up. I would think this way for many years.

When I started to understand what was going on, I became so angry with my parents. I felt all my family were at fault for not saving me. Even though they knew nothing about what happened, I felt they should have known at the time. In my mind, I couldn't understand how they could not know.

Many signs were exhibited, some of which were bed-wetting and nightmares. Before I was not scared of the dark, but after the abuse started, I became afraid of my own shadow. I also became withdrawn.

Chapter Three

It was at the age of fourteen when I first discovered alcohol. I found out that when I drank this stuff, I could forget, even if it were for just for a couple hours. But, of course, it was a delusion. As soon as I was sober again, everything came flooding back into my head, the devil's words were even louder, and those demons' roots were deeper into my soul. So I drank as often as I could. What I did not realize was this is just what the demons ordered. The delusion was that alcohol was helping me, but, indeed, it was making me much worse, and I was becoming ever more lost in that fog.

When one starts to stumble and fall in his or her fog of delusion, many people condemn them instead of trying to see why and working to help the one who has fallen.

I was almost sixteen when I was baptized at a local church. I thought it was what I needed. It was exactly what I needed but at the time, those demons attacked me so hard I did not stay in church exceptionally long. With my lack of understanding, and the church neither having a safety net or teachings for new Christians, I quickly slipped back into my darkness, my pain, my despair, my depression, and my brokenness.

In my mind, I was good at hiding my pain. My parents chalked it up to teenage rebellion. My grades were decent, but inside, my soul was in so much pain, I felt as if I were dying, and at times, I could barely breathe.

I started to drink as often as I could and, if even it was just for a very brief moment, the pain seemed to be gone. While I was drinking, I was sexually active. Drunk was the only way to give the men what they wanted. All men wanted to do was to use girls sexually, right? My mind was so messed up.

All this while the demons were whispering in my ear.

"You are no good."

"You are evil."

"You are a drunk."

"God doesn't even want you around."

"You are not a pretty person."

"You are insane."

"No one wants you."

And I believed them.

I want you to know this is often the case when one is broken and walking in the dark fog. We all believe what the devil whispers in our ears, and we sink deeper and deeper into despair. It is much easier to believe that we are bad people than it is to believe we are good people. It is easier to believe all the abuse we endured was our fault.

I got pregnant just before I turned seventeen. Of course, he was conceived while I was intoxicated. So I dropped out of school and went to Texas. I gave birth to a little boy the following year. At first, I was happy, then those little demons came back into my head. Now not only was I a teenage mother but I was also a high school drop out with no future. Wow, was I in a mess. I came home Christmas the same year. I needed my parents to help me.

My sweet little boy needed surgery on his eyes due to a genetic defect. He had his first one at thirteen months old and the second one at eighteen months old. Even though the doctors reassured me it was not my fault, I did not believe them. I felt it was my fault because I was such a bad person. I *knew* it was the alcohol. And, of course, the demons confirmed it with their whispers. My depression became even deeper.

I would walk to work, it was about two miles one way. One day, a man stopped to see if I needed a ride. I didn't know him but got in the car. He took me out in the middle of nowhere, and I thought I was going to die. I don't know how but I got away from him. I was so scared. I had to walk about ten miles to get home in the dead of night. I prayed the whole way.

I did not realize until years later that God was there watching over me and protecting me.

When I was nineteen, I married the man who I thought I was going to grow old with. Fourteen months later, I gave birth to my second son. Two years after he was born, I gave birth to my daughter. I love my children! I worked hard and took care of them. Among all the demons I was fighting, the demon of depression was the worst. Depression can make you go to dark places.

My marriage fell apart, and at twenty-six, I was a single mother with three children and my now nine-year-old son needed a third eye surgery.

I was overwhelmed. I was scared. I felt like a failure. What was wrong with me? Why wasn't I a good person? Why did everything always seem to fall apart in my life? How and why did I find a child molester to marry?

I started drinking a little heavier than usual.

It was then I "felt" Satan put his hand on my shoulder and loudly whisper to me. He told me that, indeed, I was *not* a good person. How could I be a good person, right? Look who I chose to marry! Satan wanted me to follow in his shadow. I believed all his lies.

I was bad. I was a no-good drunk. I was a bad mother. I was not a good person. I did not deserve to live.

Bitterness was consuming my heart.

I tried getting high but smoking pot made me think too much and when I came down, it just made my depression much worse.

Also at the age of twenty-six, I found myself working two jobs to try to make ends meet. I drank on the weekends to drown my "sorrows."

It was so hard. I did not realize it at the time but I was wallowing in my own self-pity. I just wanted to die. At one point, I took a whole bunch of pills. My mother quietly watched over me until I awoke two days later. She told me that I needed to seek counseling. She thought it was because I was recently divorced.

I took a good look at my life, and I *started* to realize I had a lot to live for. My attitude *started* changing, as did my gratitude. The reason for this was I started realizing all my decisions were mine. I started to realize that I was responsible for all my decisions, and I was also responsible for who I chose to influence my decisions. I saw all my blessings. It was these blessings that got me through to almost thirty.

These feelings were short lived.

I would like to say the above realization took many years to mature in my heart. I was like a child really. I was actually just starting to understand these things. It seems nothing can be fixed overnight, or can it?

Chapter Four

I was twenty-eight when I first started counseling. For the first time, I was able to tell someone what had happened. I had to stop going due to my work schedule and children; my counselor did encourage me to talk, but it would be a few more years before I really could talk. I slipped back into my depression, my chaos, and my fog.

When I turned twenty-nine, I got married. And we lived together seven out of the twelve years we were married. He drank a lot more than me, and he became abusive. This was a harsh lesson for me to learn.

But didn't I deserve this treatment? After all, I was not a good person, right? I had not been a virgin since I was seven. Good men were only for good women and vice versa, right? I had been judged quite harshly by religious and non-religious people alike. Weren't they all correct?

It was in these seven years that I found my way out of the fog, out of the darkness. This was when I could see the wound for what it was and started to heal.

I started counseling again, but this time, it was with a different look on life. I was not a victim. I was a survivor. I was no longer looking down on myself but for the first time, I was looking up. But still something was not right in my life.

Depression still loomed close by, and it would consume me every chance it got.

Then one day, I remember there was a lot of stuff on my mind. I felt I was living in a mentally chaotic state. Nothing was going right. I had been crying, my life had been just awful. I had been called to the school to talk to the principal about two of my children. I felt as if my life had me against a wall. So I decided to take a shower. Just a little break to see if my mind would stop reeling out of control. After my shower, I opened the curtain to get my towel and dry off. Across from the shower was a full-length mirror. I saw myself for the first time in a totally new light. It was then that I heard a voice from within. It was a small voice; it was speaking to me.

"Do you want your children to go through the things you have gone through?" it said.

I said, "No."

"Do you want them to follow in *your* footsteps?"

Trembling now, I said, "No."

"I can help you! There is nothing you can do about yesterday, *but* today, you can start over!"

"I love you!" I shouted.

"Please come back to me."

I then started to cry!

When I realized the voice talking to me was God, I was overwhelmed. I mean, God was telling me I was good. He could help *me*. For most of my life, I felt dirty, I felt less than human, I felt like a bad person. There were times I even felt evil. There was no judgement in His voice, no condemnation, just pure love and acceptance.

God reminded me of the words my granddaddy spoke when I was four.

I was and I am a child of God!

Immediately I dropped to my knees, soaking wet, and cried out for forgiveness, for mercy, and for salvation. My outlook changed; my whole life changed for the better! My depression started shrinking. It was what some would call an aha moment or an epiphany. I call it *God.*

Even though I read the Bible, I'd never really studied it. But I started studying. I had a pep in my step that I'd never had before. It was the surrender in my bathroom that helped me start a new walk in life. It all started with my change in the way I was thinking. The way I needed to see life was what brought me to that place on my bathroom floor and brought me back to counseling.

Looking back, I can see how God had His hand on me all my life. I can see how He had been dealing with me. I was so caught up in my chaotic fog that I either could not or would not hear Him.

The demons I was dealing with were not done with me. As a matter of a fact, they hit me harder. The devil is a deceiver. He will try to make you think things are not real. He will try to convince you that he still has you and

God is a liar. He even tries to whisper in my ear from time to time still, and his little demons of depression and low self-esteem try to come over me but now I *know* I am redeemed!

I say, "Satan, you have no power over me anymore!"

I started studying the Bible and praying. I finally found an at-home Bible study Christian congregation. The place was very conservative, and as a young Christian, it was exactly what I needed. All the parents there homeschooled their children, which was an added plus since I had recently started homeschooling my children. It was a great group. We would have Bible study, or "home church" as we called it, every Sunday and potluck afterward. This is when the children would play while the adults would talk and edify one another. This group kept me focused on God and taught me and my children to be overcomers.

During this time, I had been praying for the salvation of my husband but he decided to leave. I feel God was dealing with him, but he had demons to fight on his own.

It was a little while after my bathroom conversion when the demon of bitterness reared its ugly head. This was a difficult demon to get over. I prayed and prayed, then one day, God showed me that to be free of this bitterness, I needed to forgive the man who raped me, who ricocheted my life in all different directions. I was having a hard time with this, and this demon of bitterness was gaining strength over my life.

So many emotions were going through my heart. I felt anger, hatred, vulnerability, shame, but most of all, fear. I told God I did not think I could do this. How could I forgive anyone who had done so much damage?

Bitterness is not a gift of God; it is a demon of Satan.

God was telling me, in His sweet, small voice in my heart, that I had to forgive in order to be free from this demon of bitterness. Otherwise, I could not grow. God told me He would be with me.

It took me a few weeks, and not to mention a lot of prayer, to be able to muster up the courage to meet with this man and talk about this. When I decided to go, I kept wondering about what I would say and how I would even approach the subject. God told me not to worry about it; I would be given the words to say. I tried to believe Him.

Isn't it weird that we doubt the words of God but we believe the words of Satan?

I found out he was a resident in a nursing home not far from where I lived; he was in the last stages of colon cancer. I was also told he had dementia but did not know to what extreme. So as I traveled to the nursing home, I prayed for the strength and courage to do what I needed to do. When I finally arrived, I found out which room he was in, then suddenly, my guts started to twist. I was so nervous. I could do this. *I do not have the strength,* I thought. But God knew how much strength I had.

I started to walk down the hall where his room was, and it seemed the hallway started to elongate. When I arrived at his room, I knocked on his door and walked in.

I was surprised at what I saw. Lying in the bed was a frail old man. Suddenly, the bitterness, fear, shame, and all the other wildly negative emotions I was feeling melted away. All I felt was pity for this sick, frail, old man.

This day he did not seem to show any signs of dementia. He was lucid. He knew who I was. He asked about my parents, and we had a bit of small talk. (He had been married to a distant relative who had passed away years earlier.)

I was there for a few minutes, and when I was ready to leave, I looked at him and said, "What you did to me when I was a child, I forgive you and am praying for your salvation."

Tears welled up in his eyes and spilled down his cheeks. I also started to cry and quickly left the nursing home. By the time I got to the car, I was sobbing.

I do not know the exact day he died, but I do know it was within the month after I came to visit. I do not know if he ever asked God for forgiveness, but I do pray he did, I really do.

The day I visited him was the day I left all the burdens, including bitterness, at the altar of forgiveness. This was also the day I realized what the true meaning of forgiveness meant.

Forgiveness means letting go! We have to let go so we can grow!

Chapter Five

I was finally free!

It has been over twenty years since my bathroom experience. Have I made mistakes since then? Yes. Have I doubted? Yes. Have I listened to the whispers of those little demons? Of course, I have.

But, with prayer and study, I have become stronger in my walk with God.

I do want you to know, when I was walking in darkness, I did not constantly drink and bad things did not always happen to me. However, I did feel bad was looming over me like a dark cloud, and it was because of the following:

- I was in darkness.
- I was often in despair.

- I was wallowing in my depression.
- I was drowning in my self-pity.
- I thought little or nothing of myself.
- I was deep in sin.
- I was dishonoring my family.
- I was dishonoring me.
- I was dishonoring God.

My focus before my bathroom conversion was on my fog and my pain, which caused my chaos. I believed every bad thing whispered about me. My thoughts were not on God and a better life. Instead, they were on self-loathing and self-pity.

Looking back, I can see there were good things my life, and I thoroughly believe if it were not for those good things, I would not have survived.

There were also beacons in my life, great lighthouses in my fog to help guide me. Most of those beacons were people praying for me. Most of whom I did not even know.

My children were some of those beacons. I have since asked forgiveness from them because of my behavior and my darkness. Thankfully, they forgave me.

God sent men and women to pray for me; they were great beacons of lights and were there to offer hope and sow seeds in my life, and those seeds finally took hold. Even though I do not know who most of these people were, I genuinely believe their prayers helped me get to the place I am today. For that I am grateful.

I went on to nursing school and graduated when I was forty-nine years old. Before I went to school, I was a foster parent for about seven years. Without all of the prayers in my life, I don't know if I would have ever accomplished these things. I am grateful to God for my salvation.

The seeds these great lights sowed finally took hold and sprouted on a rock, and the roots broke that rock into many pieces to get to that good soil underneath that God had prepared before my birth.

Jeremiah 1:5 (KJV) says, "Before I formed thee in the belly I knew thee; and before thou camest forth out of the womb I sanctified thee, and ordained thee a prophet unto the nations."

I am not a prophet by any means. The above scripture tells me that God knew me before I was born.

As I said earlier, the devil starts attacking God's children before birth if we let him. If he could have all of us murdered, he would. But he cannot, so he will try to break us so we feel hopeless. The earlier he can send his demons to wreak havoc on our lives, the easier it is for him to take control and we will remain in sin. We will always feel we are not good enough for God, or mad at God, or even deny Him. The devil will pervert our thinking in a way that we will cause us to ask ourselves how a good God can allow His children to suffer.

The devil will do all he can to block our way to God.

Remember, the devil does not know the heart of God. So he does not always know who God intends to be preachers, evangelists, teachers, apostles, healers, or missionaries. Remember Bethlehem. He damages, maims, or kills as many as he can.

Satan and his demons are destroyers.

I want you to remember that the devil *will* come in many disguises and, if we let him, he will cause us to fight among one another. Humans do not forget the bad that we have done. At times, I will hear whispers about my past and even doubt my change.

When I hear this, I pray that God will open my eyes and ears to allow me to understand how the devil is using and trying to destroy me.

Remember, dear reader, if you ever feel the demon of gossip come over you, just say, *"Get behind me Satan! You have no power over me! I am a child of the Most High God!"*

Conclusion

I wanted to tell my story, not to boast but to show that anyone can make their way to God and to salvation. Each and every life is worth saving. God is our saving grace.

I want you to know that I was not worthy to wash Jesus's feet. But the day I fell to my knees in the shower, I washed His feet with my tears and dried them with my thankfulness.

I was not worthy to touch the hem of His garment. But I did when I walked into that nursing home and forgave the man who raped me. Once I forgave him, once I let go, the wound created, which issued spiritual blood all those years ago, was healed and the bitterness was gone.

We can just look at the world to see the havoc Satan and his demons have done. When we go out to the highways and byways teaching, preaching, and ministering, I want us to remember to strive to understand the following:

- Why is this human being where they are in life?
- Why are they spiritually broken?
- Why are they in spiritual pain?
- Why are they emotionally distraught?
- Why are they bitter?

Here are a few questions to ask ourselves when we are ministering:

- What has caused their darkness, their chaotic fog?
- How can we help them heal?
- How can we help them on their journey into the arms of the Holy Spirit?
- Will we be that beacon of light they so desperately needed?
- Will we be the city set upon a hill?

- Will we be the lit candle in the world of darkness?
- Will we be sowing seeds, cultivating the ground, working with God to keep the weeds at bay?
- Will it be easier to dismiss them as just a sinner and trashy?

For all have sinned, and come short of the glory of God. (Romans 3:23 KJV)

Sin is dishonor. I have dishonored myself and those around me. I have dishonored God.

I now have to make the following decisions:

- Am I going to honor God by ministering?
- Am I going to dishonor God by not being obedient?
- Am I going to dishonor other people by putting them down?
- Am I going to honor God by lifting His people up?

> For God so loved the world, that he gave his only begotten Son, that whosoever believeth in Him should not perish, but

have everlasting life. For God sent not His Son into the world to condemn the world; but that the world through Him might be saved. (John 3:16–17 KJV)

This is my commandment, That ye love one another, as I have loved you. (John 15:12 KJV)

Judge not, and ye shall not be judged: condemn not, and he shall not be condemned: forgive and ye shall be forgiven. (Luke 6:37 KJV)

Then saith He unto His disciples, "The harvest truly is plenteous, but the labourers are few." (Matthew 9 :37 KJV)

Therefore, said he unto them, the harvest truly is great, but the labourers are few: pray ye therefore the Lord of the harvest, that he would send forth labourers into his harvest. (Luke 10:2 KJV)

Brethren, if a man be overtaken with a fault, ye which are spiritual, restore such an

> one in the spirit of meekness; considering thyself, lest thou also be tempted. Bear ye one another's burdens, and so fulfil the law of Christ. (Galatians 6: 1–2 KJV)

Understanding the why is the key to a successful godly ministry!

Printed in the United States
by Baker & Taylor Publisher Services